P9-ECR-198

DESTINATION
SATURN

GILES SPARROW

PowerKiDS
press

New York

Published in 2010 by The Rosen Publishing Group
29 East 21st Street, New York, NY 10010

© 2010 The Brown Reference Group Ltd

All rights reserved. No part of this book may be reproduced in any form
without permission in writing from the publisher, except by a reviewer.

U.S. Editor: Kara Murray

Picture Credits
Key: t – top, b – below, c – center, l – left, r – right. NASA: 10, 17, 27t,
28t, ESA 12, 28b, JPL 6, 8, 9, 11, 16-17, 19, 21t, 21b, 22b, 23t, 23b, 25t,
25b, 26b, 27b, JSC 6-7, Karl Kofoed 22t, MSFC 13; Photos.com: 18, 26t;
Science Photo Library: Julian Baum 20-21, Lynette Cook 29, Mark Garlick
2-3, 14-15, 24-25; Shutterstock: Anastasiya Igolkina TP, George Toubalis
2, 4

Front cover: NASA: bl; Shutterstock: Anastasiya Igolkina c; Back cover:
Shutterstock: Anastasiya Igolkina; Backgrounds: NASA.

Library of Congress Cataloging-in-Publication Data

Sparrow, Giles.
  Destination Saturn / Giles Sparrow. — 1st ed.
      p. cm. — (Destination solar system)
  Includes index.
  ISBN 978-1-4358-3447-7 (lib. bdg.) — ISBN 978-1-4358-3461-3 (pbk.) —
ISBN 978-1-4358-3462-0 (6-pack)
  1. Saturn (Planet)—Juvenile literature. I. Title.
  QB671.S628 2010
  523.46—dc22

                                              2009002619

Manufactured in China

CONTENTS

>>>>>>> >>>>>>>

WHERE IS SATURN?

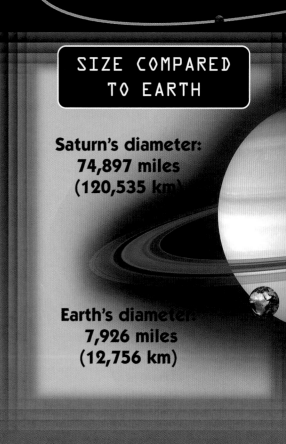

Saturn is the most distant planet we can see with the naked eye. It is famous for its beautiful and mysterious rings.

For centuries, Saturn was the farthest-known planet. The invention of the telescope in the seventeenth century then led to the discovery of Uranus, Neptune, and Pluto, the dwarf planet.

Saturn is a **gas giant**—one of the huge outer planets made almost entirely of gas. It is the second-largest planet and could swallow Earth nearly 1,000 times over.

Like all the planets, Saturn moves around the Sun along a path called an **orbit**. The time it takes to complete one orbit is the length of

SIZE COMPARED TO EARTH

Saturn's diameter:
74,897 miles
(120,535 km)

Earth's diameter:
7,926 miles
(12,756 km)

DISTANCE FROM THE SUN

Saturn is the sixth planet and the second of the giant outer planets. They are made of gas and ice. The four inner planets are made of rock. The dwarf planet Pluto is made of ice.

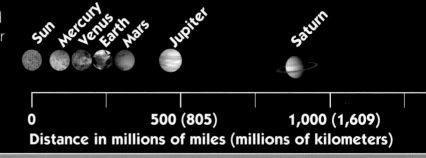

Sun   Mercury Venus Earth Mars   Jupiter   Saturn

0   500 (805)   1,000 (1,609)

Distance in millions of miles (millions of kilometers)

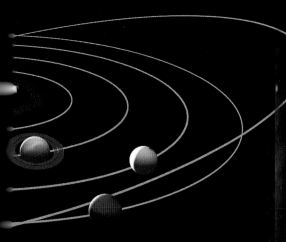

The solar system is made up of the Sun, the planets, and the asteroid belt—a ring of rocks that orbits between Mars and Jupiter.

...he planet's year. Because Saturn is ...early ten times farther from the Sun ...han Earth, its orbit is much longer ...nd its year is about 30 Earth years.

...he distance from Earth to Saturn ...hanges constantly, depending on ...he positions of both planets in their ...rbits. Saturn is closest to us when it ...nes up with Earth on the same side ...f the Sun, which happens every ...5 years. This is the time that your **mission** to Saturn is set to begin.

Getting to Saturn

The time it takes to reach Saturn depends on how you travel and on the positions of Saturn and Earth in their orbits when you set off.

Distance from Earth to Saturn
Closest	793 million miles (1.28 billion km)
Farthest	979 million miles (1.58 billion km)

By car at 70 miles per hour (113 km/h)
Closest	1,292 years
Farthest	1,595 years

By rocket at 7 miles per second (11 km/s)
Closest	3 years, 7 months
Farthest	4 years, 5 months

Time for radio signals to reach Saturn (at the speed of light)
Closest	1 hour, 11 minutes
Farthest	1 hour, 28 minutes

Uranus

Neptune

Pluto

2,000 (3,218) 2,500 (4,023) 3,000 (4,828) 3,500 (5,633)

GETTING CLOSER

Your mission to Saturn is about to begin. The journey there and back will last more than 20 years.

COMING INTO VIEW

From Earth, Saturn looks like a large yellow star. With good binoculars, it is just possible to make out the rings, which give the planet a lumpy shape. As your spaceship gets closer, the rings look like handles.

FIRST LOOK

The rings appear to get narrower and then almost vanish from view as your spaceship swings around the planet before going into orbit. They must be very thin. Saturn itself is a bright, cream-colored ball. You notice that it is not a perfect sphere—it bulges at the **equator**.

Your spacecraft is large enough to be your home for 20 years. Its engines burn slowly, but over the years you reach enormous speeds.

CLOUD SWIRLS

You can also see details on Saturn itself. Bands of color wrap around the planet, a bit like Jupiter's stripes. There are also several white blobs, including a large one close to the equator. However, you cannot see any land—Saturn is just a sea of clouds.

SEPARATE SECTIONS

Finally you reach orbit and see Saturn in all its glory. The bright rings stretch many thousands of miles (km) into space. In places they are broken by dark gaps. As you get closer you see even more gaps, and finally you realize that there are actually thousands of separate rings around Saturn.

By measuring the time that cloud features take to go around the planet, you can time Saturn's **rotation**. It turns out to be just 10 hours, 14 minutes. Saturn is spinning so rapidly that the fastest-moving areas near the equator are bulging outward and giving the planet its squashed shape.

SATURN'S RINGS

Even from close up, Saturn's rings look solid, but this is just a trick of the eye. They are made from millions of lumps of rock and ice.

DANGER!

You decide to take a look at the rings and steer toward their outer edge. As you get closer, you get scared. You have misjudged where the rings end. The region ahead of the spaceship is glowing slightly. There must be a very faint outer ring, and you are heading straight into it!

The ice and rock in each ring orbit Saturn along the same path.

Astronomers think
that Saturn's rings
might be the remains
of a smashed moon.

CIRCLES OF ICE

When the almost invisible faint outer
ring is included, Saturn's rings extend
an incredible distance. They are about
75 times wider than Earth!

You put on your space suit and take a
space walk to check the ship for
damage. The ship is covered in dents
but is still safe. A sample scoop has
collected some of the material from the
outer ring. It is tiny pieces of dusty ice
and specks of grit.

BUMPY RIDE

Preparing yourself for **impact**, you watch as
the main rings closer to Saturn get so narrow
that they are just a straight line across the
sky. You are now in the ring, and the ship is
shaking and rattling as though it is going
through a hailstorm. Then suddenly the
shaking stops, you have made it through.

A BALL
OF GAS

This computer image of Saturn has been colored to show the bands of cloud in the atmosphere more clearly.

It is time to take a look at the planet itself. You move close enough to make out details in the pale, swirling clouds.

ALL THE WAY DOWN

Saturn's clouds are not just a thin blanket over a solid planet, like the clouds of Earth and Venus. Instead, Saturn is gas nearly all the way through, with just a small solid **core** at the center.

It is hard to get an idea of the size of Saturn from orbit, but the planet is enormous. It is nine times wider than Earth.

It is about 75,000 miles (121,000 km) across but only about 68,000 miles (109,000 km) tall. That makes it the least round planet in the **solar system**.

IN THE SUMMER TIME

You have arrived at the start of summer in Saturn's northern hemisphere, just in time for one of the planet's most spectacular events. A huge storm has broken out and s spreading around the planet as you watch. Like a thundercloud on Earth, the storm is caused by warm air rushing upward. However, this storm is not just bigger than a storm on Earth, t is bigger than Earth itself!

The storm looks white because icy crystals are freezing at the top. Ferocious winds of around 1,000 miles per hour (1,600 km/h) have blown into one side of the storm, giving it an arrow shape. As you watch, the winds blow huge masses of white clouds off the storm and send them hurtling across the planet, stirring up Saturn's calm stripes.

SATURN'S SEASONS

Because Saturn spins on a tilt, it has seasons. Summer happens in the part of Saturn that is tilted toward the Sun, and winter happens in the part that is tilted away. Saturn's seasons are far longer than those of Earth. Because Saturn's year lasts about 30 times longer than ours, summer there lasts eight Earth years!

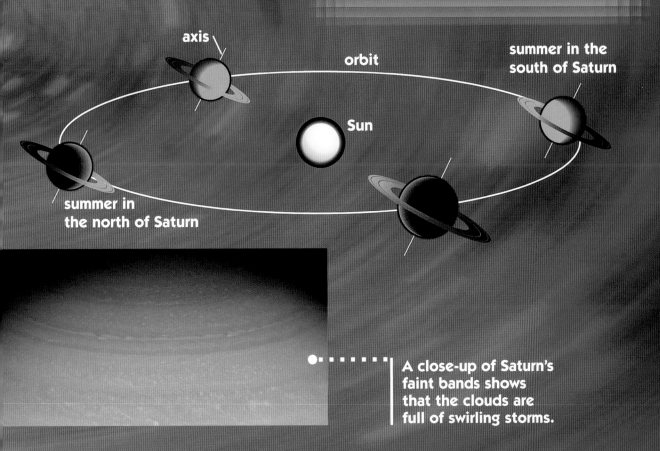

axis

orbit

summer in the south of Saturn

Sun

summer in the north of Saturn

A close-up of Saturn's faint bands shows that the clouds are full of swirling storms.

RAPID ROTATION

Saturn spins quickly. The Sun is up for just five hours before the short night begins. The daytime **temperature** at the cloud tops is –290°F (180°C), but this hardly drops as you cross to the night side. Heat from inside Saturn must be keeping the temperature steady.

CLOUD TOUR

Next, you take a flight through the planet's upper **atmosphere**. Flashes of lightning light up the towering clouds.

Then you notice a strange colorful glow in the southern sky. This is Saturn's **aurora**. An aurora is caused by the **solar wind**, a stream of **charged particles** that continually pours out of the Sun. Particles from the solar wind get trapped in Saturn's **magnetic field** and sucked toward the **poles**, where they smash into air **molecules** and release their **energy** as light.

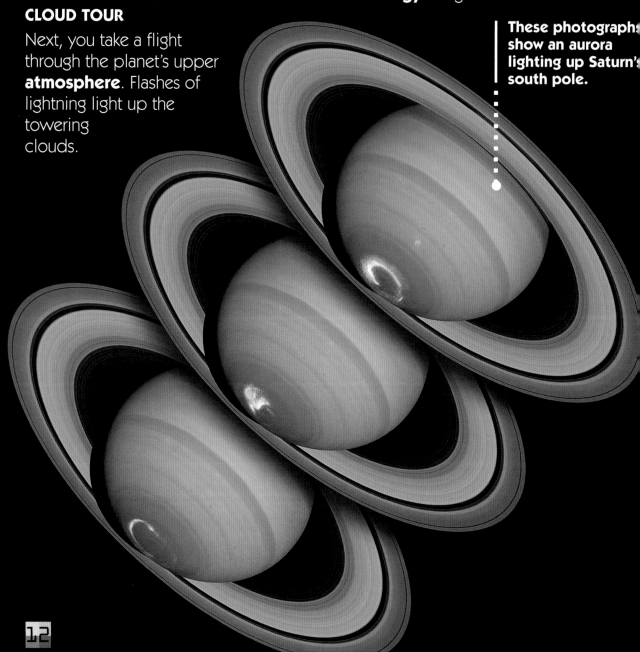

These photographs show an aurora lighting up Saturn's south pole.

WHAT'S INSIDE
SATURN?

Saturn has no solid surface to explore. Instead, you decide to drop a **probe** to study the planet's atmosphere.

Saturn's magnetic field traps a belt of deadly radiation (blue) around the planet.

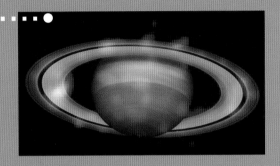

THIN GIANT

The first discovery is a big surprise. Although Saturn is much bigger and heavier than Earth, its **gravity** is slightly weaker than the gravity on the surface of Earth. That means the material inside Saturn must be spread out very thinly, making Saturn the least **dense** planet in the solar system.

THE FLOATING PLANET

Saturn has the lowest density of any planet. If you had a large enough bathtub, Saturn would float in it (right)! The low density explains the planet's bulges. Saturn's weak gravity cannot pull its gases into a sphere, so the fast-spinning equator bulges out farther than it does on other gas planets.

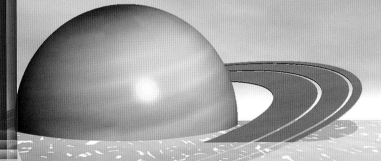

The probe's journey into Saturn will be a one-way trip. In the end, it will be crushed by the planet's thick atmosphere.

INTO THE UNKNOWN

The probe drops into the pale clouds and the video feed gets hazy. Suddenly, the probe breaks into clear air and you get another surprise. Directly below are Saturn's inner clouds. They are very colorful. Swirling patterns of blue, red, brown, and creamy white completely cover the planet, while overhead the Sun shines softly through the yellow haze. The probe's sensors tell you that the air is mainly **hydrogen**.

CRUSHING FALL

As your probe goes down farther, the pictures it sends back get darker as the atmosphere gets thicker. The **pressure** increases and the air gets steadily hotter. Before long, the signal dies as the probe is crushed by the hot and thick atmosphere.

Even though Saturn is the least dense planet, no probe could get all the way to its center. **Astronomers** have to figure out what the inside is like by using what they know about the gases that make up Saturn. Deep inside, the gases are squeezed and heated a great deal and behave in unusual ways.

hydrogen air

hydrogen and
helium ocean

metallic hydrogen

core

This is a diagram of
the different layers
inside Saturn. The
surface is colder than
any place on Earth,
while the center is as
hot as the Sun!

STRUCTURE

If you could cut Saturn open and look inside, you
would see that the outer cloud layers are 250
miles (400 km) deep. Below the clouds, the
planet's inside is a much calmer place. It is a
steadily spinning ball of hydrogen, divided into
several shells. Closest to the surface is an outer
layer of hydrogen air. This merges into an ocean
of liquid hydrogen, which also has **helium** in it.

MAGNETIC LIQUIDS AND HOT ROCK

Toward the bottom of the ocean, the hydrogen is
squeezed and heated by the weight of all the gas
and liquid above. As a result, the liquid becomes
metallic. The spinning liquid acts like a giant
magnet, generating Saturn's huge magnetic field.

In the heart of the planet is a core of solid rock,
about the size of Earth. If you could stand there,
the pressure from overhead would be a million
times greater than Earth's air pressure. The
temperature is 9,000°F (5,000°C), as hot as
the surface of the Sun!

HOW SATURN FORMED

As you return to a higher orbit far above Saturn, you wonder how this beautiful and unusual planet formed.

The Sun and the rest of the solar system formed from a cloud that was itself formed when a giant star exploded several billion years ago.

IN THE CLOUD

All the planets formed about 4.5 billion years ago, from a huge disk of gas, ice, and dust that was left behind after the Sun had formed. All the gases were pushed away from the Sun by the solar wind. The heavy dust and metal stayed closer in and made the four rocky planets. The inner part of the cloud was also too hot for ices to remain frozen, so most ice was found in the outer region.

Saturn formed as ice and dust particles collided and gradually stuck together to form a solid core. The gravity of the core gradually pulled a thick covering of gases around it.

RING FORMATION

You fly over the rings again to find clues as to how they formed. The rings have ice blocks as big as houses in them. Yet the rings are still unbelievably thin, just 33 feet (10 m) thick in places.

The rings lie in an area where the planet's gravity would tear apart any larger object in orbit and then stop the **debris** from clumping together to form a moon.

SMASHED MOON?

So are the rings made from debris left over from when Saturn formed? Astronomers do not think this is true because there is too much material in the rings. If Saturn had always had rings, most of the rocks and ice in them would have fallen into the planet by now. There would be only a little left in orbit.

Saturn's rings must have formed more recently than the planet. One explanation is that the rings are the remains of an icy moon that was smashed to pieces by a collision with a **comet**. Small moons within the rings probably help refill the material as pieces of ice are chipped from their surfaces.

Saturn's rings are probably younger than the planet.

THE SATURN SYSTEM

Saturn has a large family of 18 moons, ranging from small lumps of rocks to worlds that are big enough to be planets themselves.

RING MOONS

Saturn's closest moons orbit within rings. These are called the shepherd moons because they herd the rings into shape. Astronomers have named six shepherd moons: Pan, Atlas, Prometheus, Pandora, Epimetheus, and Janus.

Saturn's many moons are made from the material left over from when the planet formed.

Saturn

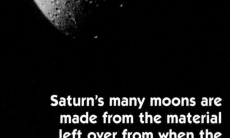

Pan

Atlas

Prometheus

Pandora

Janus

Epimetheus

Mimas

Enceladus

Calypso

Telesto

Tethys

Helene

Dione

Rhea

ICY PAIRS

The four larger moons beyond the rings come in pairs: Mimas and Enceladus are about 375 miles (600 km) across. Next are Tethys and Dione, both about 700 miles (1,100 km) across. Tethys and Dione share their orbits with much smaller moons— Telesto, Calypso, and Helene.

OUTER ZONE

Farther out, the system gets less crowded. Rhea is 940 miles (1,500 km) wide. Then comes Titan, a giant that is larger than the planet Mercury.

Beyond Titan is tiny Hyperion, then Iapetus, a strange moon roughly the size of Rhea. The last moon, Phoebe, is just 137 miles (220 km) across. It is probably an **asteroid** captured by Saturn's gravity. Phoebe moves in the opposite direction from all the other moons, in a stretched orbit that takes it millions of miles (km) from Saturn.

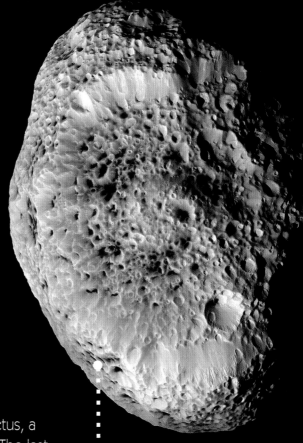

The tiny ice moon Hyperion looks like a sponge. This effect is due to dark dust on the surface being warmed by the Sun and melting holes in the moon.

Hyperion

Phoebe

Titan

Iapetus

Saturn's 18 moons are shown here to scale, except for Pan, Atlas, Telesto, Calypso, and Helene, which have been multiplied in size by five. They are shown in order, with Pan, the closest moon to Saturn, on the left.

SATURN'S MOONS

You decide to take a tour of the entire Saturn system, from the tiny shepherd moons to distant Phoebe.

KEEPING ORDER

The shepherd moons are just a few miles (km) across. However, the shepherd moons have just enough gravity to sweep up stray material from within the ring system, creating gaps between the individual rings. In this way, they "shepherd" the rings into their fixed shape. The moons' gravity sometimes also creates short-lived gaps that run across the rings, like the spokes of a bicycle wheel.

The shepherd moons are often hit by meteorites. These collisions add more chips of ice and rock to Saturn's rings.

Mimas's huge crater is named for William Herschel, who discovered the moon in 1789. . . . . . .

Herschel Crater

BIG HITTER

Now you head for Mimas, a bright white world covered with thousands of **craters**, including a giant one called Herschel. Herschel is more than 80 miles (130 km) across—nearly a third as wide as the moon itself.

IN THE CRATER

You land close to the center of the Herschel Crater and step out onto the airless surface. The ground is covered with powdery ice, and you have to wear boots with spikes to keep a grip in the very weak gravity. A quick test shows that the ice is nearly pure water. Mimas is a giant ice ball!

In the distance, you can see the huge wall of mountains that forms the crater's rim, but your view is mostly of Herschel's central mountains—peaks of solid ice 2.5 miles (4 km) high. Herschel is an impact crater, formed by a collision with a comet millions of years ago. The central mountains formed when the ground bounced back after the impact.

Saturn's moons, such as Rhea, shown here, are dwarfed by the giant planet. . . . .

Rhea

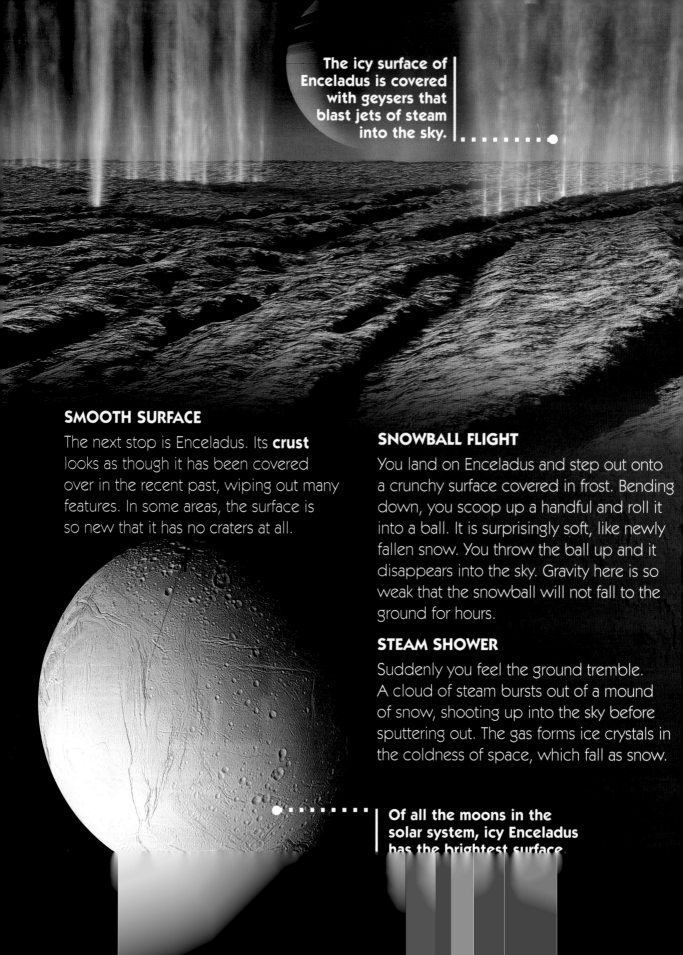

The icy surface of Enceladus is covered with geysers that blast jets of steam into the sky.

SMOOTH SURFACE

The next stop is Enceladus. Its **crust** looks as though it has been covered over in the recent past, wiping out many features. In some areas, the surface is so new that it has no craters at all.

SNOWBALL FLIGHT

You land on Enceladus and step out onto a crunchy surface covered in frost. Bending down, you scoop up a handful and roll it into a ball. It is surprisingly soft, like newly fallen snow. You throw the ball up and it disappears into the sky. Gravity here is so weak that the snowball will not fall to the ground for hours.

STEAM SHOWER

Suddenly you feel the ground tremble. A cloud of steam bursts out of a mound of snow, shooting up into the sky before sputtering out. The gas forms ice crystals in the coldness of space, which fall as snow.

Of all the moons in the solar system, icy Enceladus has the brightest surface.

HOT INSIDE

Why is Enceladus so different from nearby Mimas? Enceladus is warm enough to have liquid water and steam inside it. It is heated by the gravity of Saturn's larger moons, which pulls on the inside of Enceladus in the same way that Earth's Moon pulls on the oceans to create the tides. This process is called **tidal heating**.

ICE MOONS

Leaving Enceladus behind, you pass the other midsize moons: first Tethys, then Dione, and finally Rhea. These moons are too small to have an atmosphere. Their bright, reflective surfaces show that they are made of rock and ice. You notice that all three moons have surface gashes and signs of ancient ice **eruptions**.

Titan is so large that if it was in orbit around the Sun instead of Saturn, we would call it a planet.

ORANGE GIANT

You are now heading for Titan. As you approach it, you can see no surface detail. It just looks like an orange ball. Titan's air is orange because it has a gas called methane in it. Your instruments show that there is solid land hidden below.

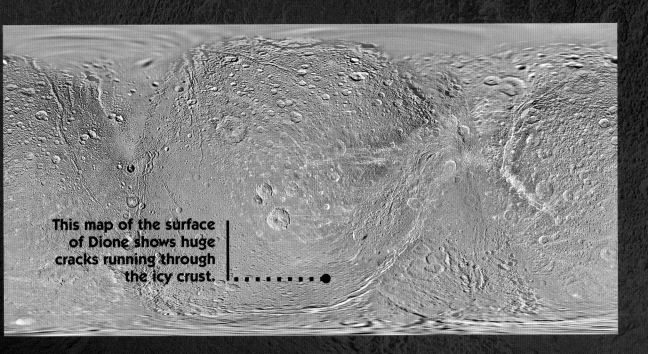

This map of the surface of Dione shows huge cracks running through the icy crust.

OILY RAIN

Taking your first walk on Titan, you can
see Saturn shining dimly through the
orange haze. The ground is wet and
slippery. It is raining, but the rain
cannot possibly be water. Titan's
surface is very cold, about −290°F
(−180°C), so water would fall as hail,
not rain. The rain puddles are thick
and greasy, like oil. It turns out that the
liquid is an **organic chemical** called
ethane. Ethane is **flammable** on Earth,
but there is no **oxygen** on Titan, so
nothing can burn. Otherwise one spark
would set the moon on fire.

ODD COUPLE

Saturn's outermost two moons are
very strange. When Iapetus was first
discovered, astronomers could see it
when it was on one side of Saturn but
not when it was on the other. The only
explanation was that Iapetus must
have a bright half and a very dark half.
As you fly past, you can see that this
is correct. The side facing forward is
covered in soot. The one facing
backward is bright ice.

**Titan has lakes and
rivers but the liquids in
them are chemicals
similar to gasoline.**

TRAPPED ASTEROID

It looks as if Iapetus is actually an icy moon that has picked up a dark coating by flying into a cloud of soot. Where could this sooty material have come from? One possible answer is revealed as you get close to Phoebe. This moon must be a late arrival in the Saturn system because it is orbiting the planet in the wrong direction. Phoebe is probably a captured asteroid. Its surface is not icy white, but sooty, like the dark side of Iapetus.

SPRAY PAINTING

Phoebe is not a perfect sphere. The surface is heavily cratered, and you can see deep cracks in it. It has clearly had a violent past. Perhaps it was torn apart and re-formed as it was captured and pulled into orbit around Saturn. Dust blasted off Phoebe by these collisions has probably coated Iapetus. Saturn's gravity pulls the dark dust inward, across the path of Iapetus.

Iapetus is covered in craters, including this 280-mile (450 km) impact basin near the moon's south pole.

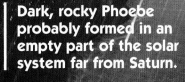

Dark, rocky Phoebe probably formed in an empty part of the solar system far from Saturn.

STUDYING SATURN

Saturn has been seen for centuries but little was known about it until the invention of the telescope.

The Italian Giovanni Cassini made a detailed study of Saturn's rings in the late 1600s.

POOR VIEW

Early telescopes gave a fuzzy view of Saturn. The rings looked like bulges. Then a few years later, the bulges disappeared, only adding to the mystery. Dutch astronomer Christiaan Huygens suggested that the bulges were flat rings in 1655. Huygens also found Saturn's main moons.

ROCKY RINGS

At first, astronomers had thought Saturn's rings were solid. Then Giovanni Cassini believed they might be made up of thousands of tiny moons. In 1895, U.S. astronomer James Edward Keeler used light from the rings to show that different segments were moving at different speeds. Cassini had been right.

PROBES ARRIVE

Many of Saturn's mysteries were solved when space probes were sent to the planet. The first probe to head for Saturn was *Pioneer 11*. It was sent off in April 1973, and it flew past Jupiter in December 1974. The probe used the planet's gravity to catapult it toward Saturn but it did not reach Saturn until September 1979. *Pioneer* took the first close-up images of the planet and the rings. It also measured Saturn's **radiation** belt and magnetic field.

Pioneer 11 flew just **13,125 miles (21,000 km) above Saturn's clouds, and then it nearly crashed into a shepherd moon!**

Voyager 1 was **sent off by a rocket in 1977. It spent three years traveling to Saturn.**

SAILING THROUGH SPACE

As *Pioneer* was flying toward Saturn, *Voyager 1* and *Voyager 2* were being sent off. They were far more advanced than the *Pioneer* probe and set out on a tour of the outer solar system. *Voyager 1* visited Jupiter and Saturn, while *Voyager 2* visited both these planets before continuing on to Uranus and Neptune. The *Voyager* probes photographed Saturn's major moons for the first time and discovered several smaller ones.

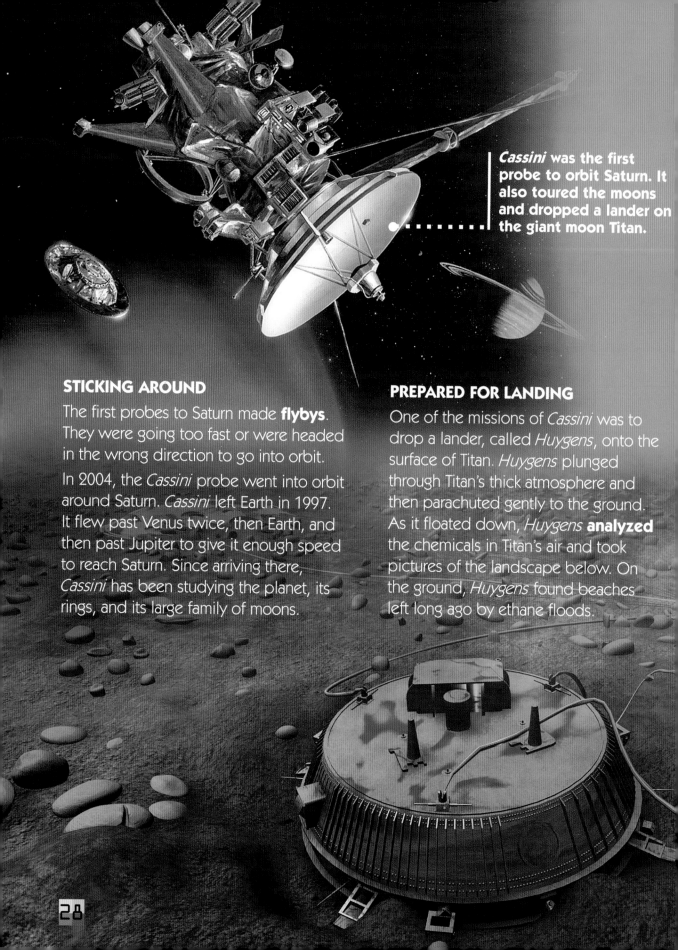

Cassini **was the first probe to orbit Saturn. It also toured the moons and dropped a lander on the giant moon Titan.**

STICKING AROUND

The first probes to Saturn made **flybys**. They were going too fast or were headed in the wrong direction to go into orbit.

In 2004, the *Cassini* probe went into orbit around Saturn. *Cassini* left Earth in 1997. It flew past Venus twice, then Earth, and then past Jupiter to give it enough speed to reach Saturn. Since arriving there, *Cassini* has been studying the planet, its rings, and its large family of moons.

PREPARED FOR LANDING

One of the missions of *Cassini* was to drop a lander, called *Huygens*, onto the surface of Titan. *Huygens* plunged through Titan's thick atmosphere and then parachuted gently to the ground. As it floated down, *Huygens* **analyzed** the chemicals in Titan's air and took pictures of the landscape below. On the ground, *Huygens* found beaches left long ago by ethane floods.

COULD HUMANS LIVE THERE?

Saturn has no solid surface on which to build a base, so astronauts would have to choose a moon on which to settle.

In five billion years, the Sun will swell up, making Earth too hot to live on. However, Titan will warm up to become a world much like Earth today.

MOON BASE

All of Saturn's moons are bitterly cold, with temperatures around −200°F (−130°C). Sunlight is so dim that solar power plants would be useless. Some other kind of fuel would be needed.

Titan might seem like a promising place for a base. The organic chemicals on Titan could be used as fuel or to make a range of other things. Ice trapped below the moon's surface could be used as a water supply or as a source of oxygen.

FIRE HAZARD

However, Titan will be a dangerous place. If oxygen was let out into the atmosphere, the organic chemicals might catch fire and turn the planet into a blazing inferno. Perhaps astronauts would find it safer to build an airtight base on one of the nearby icy moons, such as Hyperion, and make occasional trips to Titan to collect valuable materials.

GLOSSARY

analyzed (A-nuh-lyzd) Studied using scientific tests.

asteroid (AS-teh-royd) A large chunk of rock left over from when the planets formed.

astronomers (uh-STRAH-nuh-merz) Scientists who study planets and other objects in space.

atmosphere (AT-muh-sfeer) The layer of gas trapped by gravity around the surface of a planet.

aurora (uh-ROR-uh) A colorful glow in the sky caused by charged particles hitting the atmosphere.

charged particles (CHARJD PAR-tih-kulz) Tiny pieces smaller than an atom or small groups of atoms that have an electric charge.

comet (KAH-mit) A large chunk of ice left over from when the planets formed. It grows a long, glowing tail of gas and dust as it nears the Sun.

core (KOR) The center of a planet or moon where the heaviest elements have collected.

craters (KRAY-turz) Holes made in the ground when space rocks smash into a planet or moon.

crust (KRUST) The solid outer surface of a planet or moon, where the lighter elements have collected.

debris (duh-BREE) Pieces of rock, dust, ice, or other materials floating in space.

dense (DENTS) Having a lot of weight squeezed into a small space.

energy (EH-nur-jee) Something that gives an object heat or movement.

equator (ih-KWAY-tur) An imaginary line around the center of a planet, moon, or star that is located midway between the poles.

eruptions (ih-RUP-shunz) When lava or other matter oozes out of a crack in the ground or the crater of a volcano.

flammable (FLA-muh-bel) Able to burn.

flybys (FLY-byz) Missions in which a space probe passes close to a planet but is traveling too fast to go into orbit around the planet.

gas giant (GAS JY-ant) A huge planet made out of gas. Jupiter and Saturn are gas giants.

gravity (GRA-vih-tee) A force that pulls objects together. The heavier or closer an object is, the stronger its pull, or gravity.

helium (HEE-lee-um) The second-most-common element in the universe. Helium is one of the gases inside Saturn.

hydrogen (HY-dreh-jen) The simplest, lightest, and most common element in the universe. Hydrogen is the fuel that makes stars shine. It makes up most of the gas in the Sun and in Jupiter.

impact (IM-pakt) When two objects hit each other.

magnetic field (mag-NEH-tik FEELD) The region around a planet where a compass can detect the north pole.

metallic (meh-TA-lik) Like a metal, conducting electricity and being magnetic.

mission (MIH-shun) An expedition to visit a certain place in space, such as a planet or moon.

molecules (MAH-lih-kyoolz) Tiny units of matter consisting of two or more atoms joined together.

orbit (OR-bit) The path an object takes around another when it is trapped by the larger object's gravity.

organic chemical (or-GA-nik KEH-mih-kul) A chemical made up of molecules having carbon atoms in them. Methane and ethane are simple organic chemicals.

oxygen (OK-sih-jen) The invisible gas in Earth's air that living things breathe in.

poles (POHLZ) The top or bottom ends of the axis of a planet, moon, or star.

pressure (PREH-shur) A measure of how much the air pushes down on you.

probe (PROHB) A robotic vehicle sent from Earth to study the solar system.

radiation (ray-dee-AY-shun) Energy let out in rays from a source, such as the Sun. Heat and light are types of radiation.

rotation (roh-TAY-shun) How an object turns around a central point, or axis.

solar system (SOH-ler SIS-tem) The planets, asteroids, and comets that orbit the Sun.

solar wind (SOH-ler WIND) The constant stream of particles that travels out of the Sun and through the solar system at very high speed.

space walk (SPAYS WOK) Moving outside a spaceship while the ship is in space.

temperature (TEM-pur-cher) How hot something is.

tidal heating (TY-dul HEET-ing) The heating of a moon's inside as it is pulled in different directions by the gravity of its parent planet and other moons.

INDEX

A

asteroids 5, 19, 25
astronomers 9, 14, 17–18, 24, 26
atmosphere 10, 12–14, 23, 28–29
aurora 12

C

Cassini, Giovanni 26
Cassini, probe 28
clouds 7, 10–12, 14–16, 27
core 10, 15–16
crust 22–23

D

day, Saturn's 7
density 13
Dione, moon 18–19, 23

E

Enceladus, moon 18–19, 22–23

G

gravity 13, 16, 19, 20–23, 25, 27

H

Herschel crater 21
Huygens, Christiaan 26
Huygens lander 28
Hyperion, moon 19, 29

I

Iapetus, moon 19, 24–25
ice 4, 8–9, 16–17, 20–24, 29

J

Jupiter 4–5, 7, 27–28

M

magnetic field 12–13, 15, 27
Mars 4–5
Mimas, moon 18–19, 21, 23
mountains 21

O

orbits 4–8, 10–11, 16–19, 23, 25, 28

P

Phoebe, moon 19–20, 25
Pioneer 11 probe 27
poles 12, 25

probe 13–14, 27–28

R

radiation belt 13, 27
Rhea, moon 18, 19, 21, 23
rings 4, 6–9, 16–20, 26–28
rock 4, 8, 15, 17–18, 20, 23
rotation 7, 12–13

S

seasons 10–11
shepherd moons 18, 20
solar system 5, 10, 13, 16, 22, 25, 27
solar wind 12, 16
Sun 4–5, 11–12, 14–16, 19, 23, 29

T

telescope 4, 26
temperature 12, 15, 29
Tethys, moon 18–19, 23
Titan, moon 19, 23–24, 28–29

V

Voyager probes 27

WEB SITES

Due to the changing nature of Internet links, PowerKids Press has developed an online list of Web sites related to the subject of this book. This site is updated regularly. Please use this link to access the list:
www.powerkidslinks.com/dsol/saturn/